REAL WORLD ADVENTURES

REAL Animal HEROES

by Gregory N. Peters

WITHDRAWN

CAPSTONE PRESS
a capstone imprint

Trailblazers Books are published by Capstone Press,
1710 Roe Crest Drive, North Mankato, Minnesota 56003
www.capstonepub.com

Library of Congress Cataloging-in-Publication Data
Peters, Gregory N.
Real animal heroes / by Gregory N. Peters.
pages cm. -— (Trailblazers. Real world adventures)
Summary: "Shares amazing stories of brave animals that have rescued others
and saved lives"— Provided by publisher.
Includes bibliographical references and index.
ISBN 978-1-4765-8532-1 (library binding)
1. Animal heroes—Anecdotes—Juvenile literature. 2. Animal behavior--
Juvenile literature. 3. Animals—Anecdotes—Juvenile literature. 4. Pets—
Anecdotes—Juvenile literature. 5. Human-animal relationships—Juvenile
literature. I. Title.
SF416.2.P473 2014
591.5—dc23   2013029426

Editorial Credits
Christine Peterson, editor; Gene Bentdahl, designer; Eric Gohl, media
researcher; Eric Manske, production specialist

Photo Credits
AP Photo: 39, Alan Diaz, 43, Atlanta Journal & Constitution/Johnny Crawford,
35, Tetsuya Kikumasa, Yomiuri Shimbun, 12, Todd Plitt, 21; Corbis: Bettmann,
28, Reuters/X00404/Alexander Khudotioply, 11; DVIC: U.S. Air Force/Master
Sergeant Michael E. Best, 14–15, U.S. Army/Sgt. Daniel Schroeder, 32; Getty
Images: Hulton Archive/FPG, 31; Library of Congress: 4; Newscom: Europics,
26, Splash News, 9, ZUMA Press/Hector Amezcua, 7; Shutterstock: cynoclub,
19, fotostory, cover, IbajaUsap, 40, Marcel Jancovic, 17, PhotoStock10, 25, Sari
ONeal, 36, Tom Hirtreiter, 22

Printed in China by Nordica.
1013/CA21301911
029013   007739NORDS14

TABLE OF CONTENTS

Terrorists crashed a plane into Tower 2 on September 11, 2001.

CHAPTER 1

September 11

Boom! Michael Hingson heard a giant explosion. At first he didn't know what it was. It sounded like a giant bomb or an earthquake. The building started swaying. The air was filled with smoke and fire. Hingson smelled gasoline.

It was the morning of September 11, 2001. New York City had just been attacked. **Terrorists** had crashed two planes into two buildings. The World Trade Center was hit. Both towers were burning. Thousands of people were inside. They had to get out. But it wouldn't be easy. Things were smashed. The elevators had stopped working. They had to climb down the stairs. It was dark and smoky in many places. For Michael Hingson it was especially challenging. Hingson is blind.

terrorist - someone who uses violence and threats to frighten people

Guide Dogs

Michael Hingson worked on the 78th floor of the North Tower. When the plane hit, he knew he had to get out. Hingson helped everyone in his office get to safety. But he couldn't have done it alone. He had the help of his **guide dog**, Roselle.

The strong yellow Labrador retriever stayed calm. She did what she had been trained to do. She kept Hingson safe. Roselle led Hingson through the damaged office to the stairs. They began their long trip. They had to walk down 78 floors.

It was hot and hard to breathe. They managed to get out of the building. But they weren't out of danger. They had to get as far away as they could. When they were about two blocks away, they heard a frightening sound. One of the towers had begun to collapse. "It sounded like a metal and concrete waterfall," Hingson said. The air was filled with ash, dust, and other **debris**. Still, Roselle remained calm. They had a long way to go to get home. But they made it!

Roselle was an incredible hero. She lived happily with the Hingson family until her death in 2011.

debris - pieces of something that has been broken
guide dog - a dog trained to help people who are blind

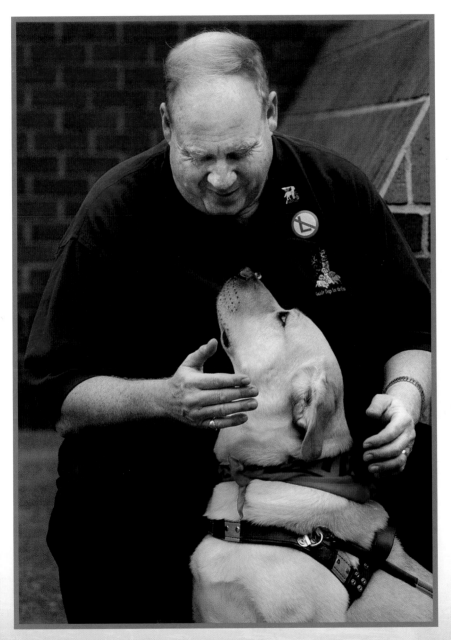

Michael Hingson and brave Roselle

Search and Rescue

There were other hero dogs that terrible day. Not all of them were from New York state. Some were not even from the United States. James Symington lived in Canada. He came to New York City to help after the planes hit. He drove 15 hours with his dog Trakr.

Symington worked with dogs as part of a **K-9** search and rescue team. Trakr had been on the team, but he stopped working when he grew older. Symington wanted him to work one more time. Trakr still had a lot of hero in him.

New York needed a lot of help. Trakr worked for hours and hours. He found many hurt people in the **rubble**. Trakr found the last **survivor**. He found her 27 hours after the buildings collapsed.

K-9 – having to do with dogs

rubble – broken items left from a building that has fallen down

survivor – someone who lives through a disaster or horrible event

James Symington and Trakr helped find survivors in the rubble.

More Heroes

More than 300 dogs searched for survivors and victims. They worked in the broken ruins of the fallen buildings.

Some dogs can help stop a disaster. These dogs are trained to find things like bombs. They use their noses to sniff for them.

In 1972 a dog named Brandy saved the day. Someone had called the airport. The person said there was a bomb on a plane. The people who worked at the airport were nervous. They brought Brandy in to look for the bomb. She was with her **handlers**.

Brandy did what she was trained to do. She was a real pro. She found the bomb just in time. It was set to go off in 12 minutes! Since that day, dogs have been used at many airports to help keep people safe.

handler – a person who trains or manages a dog for work

When scary things happen, animals can sometimes help. Dogs like Trakr, Brandy, and Roselle are trained for a job. Their job is to help their human handlers. It might mean leading the way. It might mean using their nose to track something dangerous. They all save lives. It is amazing what animals can do.

A bomb-sniffing dog checks bags.

Babu and her owner Tami Akanuma

CHAPTER 2

Natural Disasters

Thunder and lightning can be scary. But there are things more dangerous than thunderstorms. Giant tidal waves called **tsunamis** can cause major damage. This is when some animal helpers come to the rescue.

In 2011 an underwater earthquake made a huge wave. The tsunami slammed into Japan. The water came so fast that many people could not get out of the way. Many people died.

A dog named Babu was a hero that day. She is a little dog, but she helped in a big way.

Babu's owner is 83-year-old Tami Akanuma. They walked together every day. That day, they were on their walk near a hill. Babu pulled Tami up the hill. It was not something Babu usually did. But she seemed to sense the disaster to come.

By going up the hill, Babu and Tami avoided the flood waters. Babu saved her owner's life.

tsunami – a very large wave

Hurricanes can cause terrible damage. Their winds can knock down buildings. They can also cause floods. The water washes through cities. It breaks down anything in its path.

George Mitchell and his dog Frisky lived in New Orleans. In 2005 Hurricane Katrina hit the city. Mitchell's house filled with water. He and Frisky were trapped inside.

Hurricane Katrina flooded New Orleans in 2005.

Mitchell had to stay above the water. He swam in place. He held onto a mattress.

Fighting the floodwaters was hard work. Mitchell got very tired. He wanted to give up. But Frisky would not let him. Frisky licked and licked his owner. This kept Mitchell going. The two friends stayed above water for hours.

Finally the water went down. They got outside. Help was waiting. Frisky kept Mitchell alive.

15

Dog School

Some dogs are **trained** to help humans. They help when natural **disasters** or dangerous weather happens. Trainers spend months teaching the dogs how to help.

Search and rescue dogs can find lost people. Dogs have amazing noses. They can smell things humans can't. They use this sense to find people. Dogs are also smaller than humans. Being small lets them get into places people can't go.

Have you seen a police dog before? Police officers are one of the groups that train dogs to work.

Police dogs take classes with handlers. They learn to obey handlers' commands. Police dogs must listen to their handlers at all times, especially in dangerous and difficult situations.

A German shepherd trains to be a police dog.

train – to prepare by learning and practicing new skills

disaster – an event that causes much damage or suffering

A police dog must be able to work for long periods of time. The dog needs to be strong and **athletic**. A police dog must be able to jump over walls and climb fences. A police dog must be calm around a lot of people. A nervous dog won't make a good police dog.

Police dogs also receive specialty training. Some are trained to search for drugs. Some are trained to search for bombs or guns. Some police dogs are trained to track missing persons or crooks.

Some fire departments also use trained dogs. These dogs help with search and rescue missions.

Dog school isn't about math and reading. It is about saving lives. It is very important work. The dogs and their handlers are very brave.

athletic - strong, fast, and skilled; fit

Police dogs are trained to climb walls and fences.

Sensing Danger

Animals don't need training to help other animals. Some scientists have seen wild animal rescues. An animal might hear or see another animal in trouble. The animal might decide to help. The animal in danger is saved.

Adult monkeys have saved baby monkeys. Dolphins have saved other dolphins. Even tiny ants sometimes rescue each other. Scientists are studying rescue behavior in wild animals. Are these animals heroes? Some people think so!

Scarlett the cat is a good example. Scarlett was with her 4-week-old kittens in a garage. The building caught fire. Someone sounded the alarm.

A firefighter arrived and saw that Scarlett was badly burned. But all her kittens were safe. One by one, Scarlett had carried them to safety.

Newspapers printed the story. Scarlett became famous. More importantly, she found a new home for herself and her kittens.

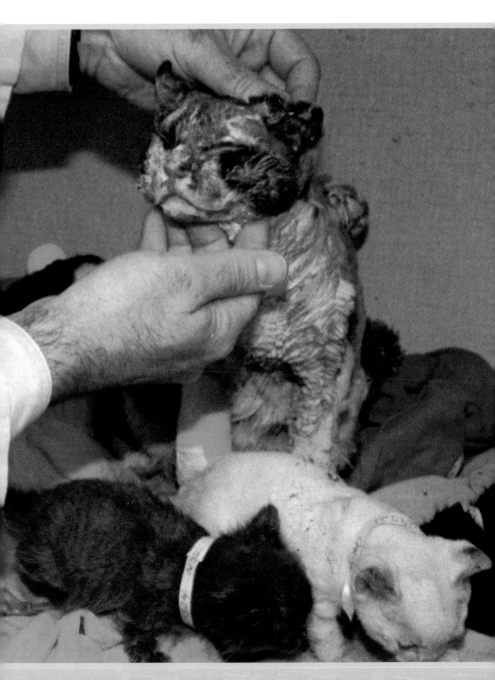

After the fire, a veterinarian checked Scarlett and her kittens.

Dolphins are smart and brave.

CHAPTER 3

Water Rescue

Imagine being on your boat when it explodes. That is what happened to Yvonne Vladislavich. She was thrown off her exploding boat. She was left alone in the ocean. She tried to stay afloat. She was sure she was going to die.

Just when Yvonne needed help, three dolphins swam by. These were not trained dolphins. They were wild, and they did something amazing. One dolphin carried the woman for hours. The others protected her from sharks.

Finally the dolphins found a **buoy** floating in the sea. Yvonne held onto the buoy, and the dolphins left her.

Soon a ship came by. It picked Yvonne up and took her home. That was an amazing story to tell her friends. She was saved by dolphins!

buoy – a floating marker in the ocean

More Dolphin Heroes

Dolphins are smart creatures. On Marco Island in Florida, a lost dog was in trouble. The dog fell into a waterway called a **canal**. The dog couldn't get out of the water. The dolphins saw the dog in trouble and came to the rescue.

The dolphins stayed with the dog for many hours. They splashed in the water the whole time. This is not something dolphins would normally do. It seems they wanted to call attention to the dog.

Some nearby people heard splashing in the canal. They came to see what was going on. They saw the dog stuck in the water and rescued him.

The people said the dolphins had been hard to miss. The noisy splashing caught their attention. The dolphins had just the right idea. And that is one lucky dog.

Splashing dolphins helped save a dog's life.

canal – a waterway joining two bodies of water so that ships can travel between them

Mila the beluga whale grabbed Yang Yun and swam her to safety.

Too Cold

Cold water can be deadly to swimmers. It almost killed Chinese athlete Yang Yun.

Yang Yun was part of a diving competition in China. She was diving in a deep, cold **arctic** pool. After her dive, Yun tried to reach the surface. She needed air to breathe. But the water was so cold that she was **paralyzed**. She was not able to move at all. In seconds Yun would have begun drowning. No one noticed she was in trouble. Thank goodness Mila was there!

Mila the beluga whale was swimming in the same pool. She saw Yun was in trouble. Mila grabbed Yun's leg in her mouth. Mila swam up and up until they reached the **surface**. When they were at the top of the water, Yun could breathe again. Somehow the whale knew just what to do.

arctic - extremely cold and wintry
paralyzed - unable to move or feel a part of the body
surface - the top of the water

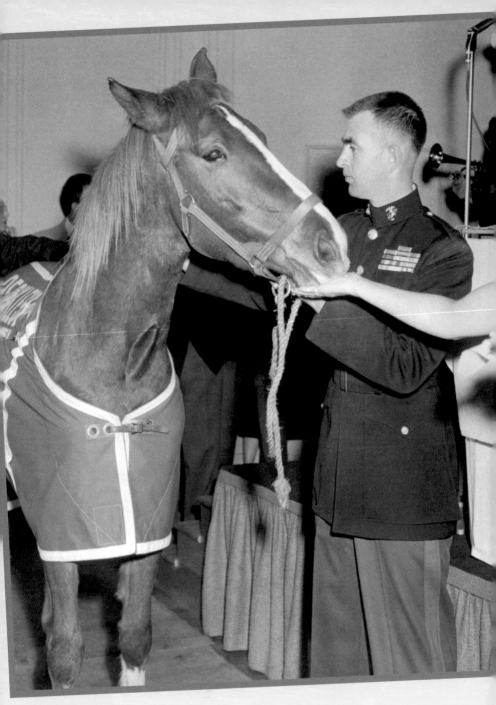

Staff Sergeant Reckless gets a treat at her birthday party.

CHAPTER 4

Wartime

Not all war heroes are soldiers and sailors. Some aren't even human. They're animals.

The Korean War took place from 1950 to 1953. Almost 37,000 Americans were killed. There were many animals that helped the soldiers. One of those brave animals was a horse named Reckless.

Reckless had a very important job. She carried supplies to the front lines. Whenever the Marines needed bullets, Reckless made a trip. At first, she was led by her handler. She walked up and down the battlefield, carrying her load. Sometimes the enemy shot at her. Luckily, she wasn't hurt.

After a while, Reckless knew the route by heart. She was able to make the trips alone. Her work kept U.S. forces safe. When the war was over, she was given special medals. The marines gave Reckless a new **rank** to show how important she was. Her new title was Staff Sergeant Reckless.

rank – status of a military member

Cher Ami

World War I (1914–1918) is known as the Great War. Many countries were involved in this war, which lasted four years. No war before had so many countries in the fight. Many soldiers were killed or hurt.

During one battle, U.S. Army Major Charles Whittlesey's men were under attack. They were trapped on a French hillside without food or bullets. Without bullets they could not fight back.

Whittlesey tied messages for help to trained carrier pigeons. Carrier pigeons would fly the messages back to base. But pigeon after pigeon was shot down. The messages never got through.

Whittlesey was running out of time. He had only one pigeon left. The bird's name was Cher Ami. In French, the name means *"dear friend."*

Cher Ami was shot as he flew away. But that did not stop this brave bird. Cher Ami kept flying—with only one leg! The message was delivered, and Cher Ami saved the day.

More than 600 carrier pigeons helped U.S. soldiers in World War I.

Fact

Cher Ami's body is on display at the Smithsonian National Museum of American History in Washington, D.C.

War Dogs

Soldiers lead dangerous lives during wartime. Every day they work to stay safe. Having animal friends beside them can help.

Many war dogs are trained for their work. They spend time in the United States learning their jobs before they go to war. Sometimes the dogs help find lost soldiers. Other times they search for explosives.

Soldiers and a trained dog board a vehicle.

It takes a special dog to be a trained war dog. Some **breeds** work better than others. Bomb squads like Labrador retrievers. Other trainers like German shepherds.

All dogs start their training as puppies. They are ready to go to work when they are two and a half years old.

War dogs live with the soldiers, and the soldiers take care of them. These dogs are an important part of the military.

Sometimes war dogs do not get any training. They are dogs without owners. These stray dogs wander onto military **bases**. In one case, some of these dogs acted like heroes. Five men are alive today because of what they did.

In 2009 three stray dogs wandered onto an American base in Afghanistan. The U.S. soldiers befriended the dogs and cared for them. The soldiers named the dogs Rufus, Target, and Sasha.

One night the dogs were barking wildly. Some of the soldiers came to see what was happening. They saw an enemy fighter. The dogs were biting him and trying to stop him. The **intruder** could not move closer. He exploded a bomb, and the dogs and men were hurt. Brave Sasha was badly hurt and died from her wounds. But all the soldiers survived. The dogs did an amazing job. They were true heroes that day.

People knew these amazing dogs deserved real homes and families. Target and Rufus were flown to the United States. There they were adopted by soldiers they saved.

base – a military-run area that houses people serving in the military

intruder – someone who enters but is not welcome

Rufus (left) and Target (right) were flown to the United States to be adopted.

Cats can be heroes too!

CHAPTER 5

To the Rescue

Emergencies can happen anytime and anywhere. Sometimes a house catches fire or someone gets hurt. What if your house was filling with smoke? Do you have a pet that would wake you up? Sometimes animals can help in emergencies. They seem to sense danger. It seems like they know what to do to help.

Glen Kruger is alive today because of his cat, Inky. Late one night, Kruger fell down the stairs to his cellar. He was badly hurt. He was losing blood and needed help. Luckily, Inky came to sit beside him. Kruger told Inky, "Go get Brenda." The cat seemed to understand.

Inky ran to the bedroom. The door was shut. Kruger's wife Brenda was asleep inside. Inky scratched and cried at the door. Brenda woke up and followed Inky to Glen. She called 911 for help. Inky was a hero!

In 1986 a 5-year-old British boy and his family went to the Durrell Wildlife Park. The little boy's name was Levan. Levan's visit started out well. Soon it became very scary.

Levan and his family stopped to see the gorillas. Male gorillas are called **silverbacks**, and Jambo was a large one. Levan and his family were looking at Jambo and the other gorillas.

A 12-foot (3.7 meter) wall kept the gorillas in the **exhibit** where they lived. When Levan's mom and dad were not looking, Levan climbed up the wall. He fell into the exhibit with the huge gorillas!

Everyone was very scared. Gorillas can be gentle. But they are very strong. If they wanted to hurt Levan, it would be easy to do. They were so big that they could hurt him without meaning to.

silverback – an adult male gorilla; one silverback leads each troop

exhibit – in area in a zoo where animals live to keep them separate from people

Jambo and Levan in the gorilla exhibit

Jambo came up to Levan. People were frightened! But Jambo didn't hurt the boy. He just sat with Levan. It looked like Jambo was protecting him. When the boy started to cry, Jambo and the other gorillas seemed to get scared. They left Levan. Soon Levan was rescued by zookeepers. It was a happy ending. From then on, Jambo was called "the Gentle Giant."

39

Stormy

Tame animals can be heroes too. Stormy was a brave horse. She helped the children in her family. The family had a 9-year-old girl named Emma. Stormy was her riding horse.

One day, Emma, her little brother, Liam, and Stormy had a very scary ride. Liam was walking and Emma was on Stormy. On the trail, a large wild pig came out of the woods. It was a male wild pig, or **boar**. They are dangerous animals.

Boars have sharp teeth called **tusks**. Boars sometimes hurt people with their tusks.

Stormy knew what to do. She used her nose to push Liam off the trail. This kept Liam away from the boar. Then fearless Stormy went back to the boar. Stormy kicked him in the mouth! The scared boar ran away. Stormy saved the day!

Boars have big, sharp teeth called tusks.

boar - a male wild pig

tusk - a long, pointed tooth

Amazing Animals!

No one is exactly sure what animals think. They cannot talk and tell us. But we know some animals do amazing things. Animal heroes save people. They save other animals too. From trained police dogs to wild dolphins, animals can be rescuers!

Have you heard about other animal heroes? What amazing animals do you know?

Cowboy, a rescue dog, on the job.

Read More

Albright, Rosie. *Police Dogs.* Animal Detectives. New York: PowerKids Press, 2012.

Burleigh, Robert. *Fly, Cher Ami, Fly!: The Pigeon Who Saved the Lost Battalion.* New York: Abrams Books for Young Readers, 2008.

Molnar, Michael. *Bottlenose Dolphins.* Life Cycles of Marine Animals. Mankato, Minn.: Smart Apple Media, 2012.

Bibliography

page 6 • http://www.guidedogs.com/site/PageServer?pagename=about_people_staffvol_bios_mhingson

page 37 • http://www.rd.com/slideshows/americas-hero-pets#slideshow=slide5

Internet Sites

FactHound offers a safe, fun way to find Internet sites related to this book. All of the sites on FactHound have been researched by our staff.

Here's all you do:
Visit *www.facthound.com*
Type in this code: 9781476585321

 Check out projects, games and lots more at **www.capstonekids.com**

Titles in This Set

Daredevils!

Looking for Lost Treasure

Real Animal Heroes

U.S. Navy SEALs Elite Force

Glossary

arctic (ARK-tik) • extremely cold and wintry

athletic (ath-LET-ik) • strong, fast, and skilled; fit

base (BEYS) • a military-run area that houses people serving in the military

boar (BOHR) • a male wild pig

breed (BREED) • a certain kind of animal

buoy (BOO-ee) • a floating marker in the ocean

canal (kuh-NAL) • a waterway joining two bodies of water so that ships can travel between them

debris (duh-BREE) • pieces of something that has been broken

disaster (dih-ZAS-ter) • an event that causes much damage or suffering

exhibit (ex-ZHIB-it) • an area in a zoo where animals live to keep them separate from people

guide dog (GYD dog) • a dog trained to help people who are blind

handler (HAND-ler) • a person who trains or manages a dog for work

intruder (in-TROOD-ur) • someone who enters but is not welcome

K-9 (KAY-nyn) • having to do with dogs

paralyze (PAYR-uh-lahyze) • unable to move or feel a part of the body

protect (pruh-TEKT) • to keep safe

rank (RANGK) • status of a military member

rubble (RUB-uhl) • broken items left from a building that has fallen down

silverback (SIL-ver-bak) • an adult male gorilla; one silverback leads each troop

surface (SUR-fiss) • the top of the water

survivor (ser-VY-ver) • someone who lives through a disaster or horrible event

terrorist (TAYR-er-ist) • someone who uses violence and threats to frighten people

train (TRAYN) • to prepare by learning and practicing new skills

tsunami (soo-NAH-mee) • a very large wave

tusk (TUHSK) • a long, pointed tooth

Index